Study Guide

Policing in America

PREPARED BY KAREN S. MILLER-POTTER
EASTERN KENTUCKY UNIVERSITY

LARRY K. GAINES / VICTOR E. KAPPELER
CALIFORNIA STATE UNIVERSITY – SAN BERNARDINO   EASTERN KENTUCKY UNIVERSITY

4TH EDITION

anderson publishing co.
2035 Reading Road
Cincinnati, OH 45202
800-582-7295
since 1887

Policing in America, Fourth Edition
STUDY GUIDE

Copyright © 2003
Anderson Publishing Co.
2035 Reading Rd.
Cincinnati, OH 45202

Phone 800.582.7295 or 513.421.4142
Web Site www.andersonpublishing.com

This Study Guide was designed to be used in conjunction with *Policing in America, 4th ed.* © 2003 by Anderson Publishing Co. (ISBN: 1-58360-539-8)

Photocopying for distribution is prohibited.

EDITOR Gail Eccleston • ACQUISITIONS EDITOR Michael C. Braswell

Contents

Note to Students

This Study Guide was created to complement *Policing in America* by Larry K. Gaines and Victor E. Kappeler. It is not designed to serve as a substitute for the textbook. You will need to read the book to fully understand the concepts, and you will need the textbook to complete portions of this Guide.

The questions and answer key provided in this Guide provide one way for measuring how well you are grasping the material.

Chapter 1
The Police in American Society

Chapter Outline

Key Concepts

Introduction
The primary shapers of the American police institution are society and government. Democratic systems of government are built upon a delicate balance between individual rights and the collective needs of members of society. Democracy includes belief in the rule of law, individualism, civil rights, human dignity, constitutionalism, social justice, and majority rule. These ideas are the foundation of the social contract which members of society entered into agreement to create the state and a government to acquire security and order.

The Government Structure and Policing
One way to distinguish types of governments is the presence of a constitution. Constitutions are political instruments designed to curb abuses of power by the government and have an administrative quality. The U.S. Constitution restricts what police officers can do when enforcing the law or investigating crime. The first 10 amendments to the constitution are the Bill of Rights and afford American citizens certain rights and protections. The United States Constitution created three branches of government: the executive, judicial, and legislative. The police fall under the executive branch.

Police in the Criminal Justice System
One of the most popular models of criminal justice actually involves two competing models: the crime control model, which emphasizes moving cases through the system, and the due process model, which places a greater emphasis on protecting citizens' rights.

Roles and Activities Performed by Police
There are four primary roles of police in American society. (1) Law enforcement; (2) Order maintenance; (3) Provision of miscellaneous services; and (4) convenience norm enforcement. While officers typically view themselves as crime fighters, their primary activities involve problem solving, law enforcement, order maintenance, and service.

Styles of Police Departments
There are three primary policing styles: watchman, legalistic, and service. Watchman style emphasizes order maintenance and crime control. Legalistic departments emphasize uniform standards and centralized bureaucracy. Service-style departments emphasize providing services to their residents.

Law Enforcement Agencies
Federal law enforcement agencies are primarily divided into two departments, the Justice Department and the Treasury Department. Justice Department agencies include: Federal Bureau of Investigation; Drug Enforcement Administration; U.S. Marshal Service; and Immigration and Naturalization Service. Treasury Department agencies include: Bureau of Alcohol, Tobacco, and Firearms; Internal Revenue Service; and U.S. Customs Service.

State Police and Highway Patrol agencies are found in different states and have different jurisdictions and responsibilities. Local law enforcement agencies include sheriff's departments, county police agencies, and municipal police departments.

Review of Key Terms

Bureau of Alcohol, Tobacco, and Firearms
case law
civil law
constitution
crime control model
democratic systems
due process model
federalism
government
legalistic style
procedural law
separation of powers
service style
Society
substantive law
U.S. Marshal Service
watchman style

1. The concept of _____ distributes authority and power among levels of government.

2. A _____ agency is likely to be found in a homogeneous middle- or upper-class community and emphasizes provision of services to residents.

3. The _____ is in the Treasury department and its jurisdiction includes explosives.

4. The regulation of social interactions arising from private, commercial, or contractual relations is done through _____.

5. _____ of government are built upon a delicate balance between individual rights and the collective needs of members of society.

6. The _____ of policing emphasizes order maintenance and crime control.

7. _____ refers to the written opinions of the courts.

8. The concept of _____ created three branches of government.

9. The responsibilities of government and the rights of citizens are detailed in a _____.

10.   The _____ of policing emphasizes centralized or bureaucratic authority and requires officers to enforce one set of uniform standards on the public.

11.   _____ refers to laws that prescribe how police officers apply substantive laws.

12.   The _____ places a high priority on moving cases through the system.

13.   The primary shapers of the American police institution are _____ and _____.

14.   The _____ is the oldest federal law enforcement agency in existence.

15.   Criminal statutes that define which behaviors are acceptable and unacceptable in our society are referred to as _____.

16.   The _____ places emphasis on protecting citizens' rights.

Chapter 2
Historical Perspectives

Chapter Outline

I.   An Overview of Policing in Ancient Times
    A.   The Birth of Civilization in Mesopotamia
    B.   Civilization in Ancient Egypt
    C.   The Rise of Greek City-States
    D.   The Roman Empire's Contribution to Policing

II.   Police Development in England
    A.   Medieval England
    B.   Early English Law Enforcement
    C.   The English Reformers
        1.   Henry Fielding
        2.   Patrick Colquhoun
        3.   Sir Robert Peel
        4.   Charles Rowan and Richard Mayne

III.   American Policing in Retrospect
    A.   Early American policing

IV.   Policing America: The Modern Era
    A.   The Political Entrenchment Phase
    B.   The Reform Efforts
        1.   Investigative Commissions
        2.   Police Administrative Reform
        3.   General Political Reform

V.   Professional Policing Comes to America
    A.   The Law Enforcement Role
    B.   The Bureaucratic Model
    C.   Science and Technology

VI.   Public and Community Relations Return to Policing

Key Concepts

Policing in Ancient Times
The police function has been a central part of government since people started creating governments. The police function was vested with the military during earlier times. Formal policing requires that societies develop four interrelated and established themes: (1) The development of a formal legal system; (2) The emergence of social differentiation; (3) The production of a surplus of material resources; (4) The emergence of the state as a form of political organization.

Police Development in England
Until the beginning of the Industrial Revolution, law enforcement in England was a local responsibility. In Medieval England, the frankpledge system provided police services. Early English law enforcement utilized watchmen and constables. The first modern police department was created in London in 1829. Henry Fielding, Patrick Colquhoun, Robert Peel, Charles Rowan, and Richard Mayne contributed to the development of the London Metropolitan Police Department.

Early American Policing
The earliest forms of policing in America were primary volunteer situations that were designed as slave patrols or night watches. Agencies across the country were developed for different reasons, for example the Pennsylvania state police was developed to assist mine owners in breaking coal strikes.

The history of American policing can be examined in terms of four phases: (1) the political entrenchment phase; (2) the reform phase; (3) the professional phase; (4) and the public and community relations phase. The political entrenchment phase was characterized by corruption. The Reform phase brought investigative commissions, internal administrative reform and political reform. The professional phase was prompted by the Great Depression and the Volstead Act or "Prohibition." This phase was an attempt to professionalize law enforcement and focus on law enforcement. The public and community relations phase was prompted by civil unrest of the 1960s and was intended to improve police/community relations.

Review of Key Terms

Bow Street Runners
Patrick Colquhoun
community relations
Constables
Henry Fielding
Hammurabi
investigative commissions
KNAPP commission
London Metropolitan Police Force
Richard Mayne
Night Watches
Pennsylvania State Police
political entrenchment
professional era
reform era
Sir Robert Peel
slave patrols
Texas Rangers
Charles Rowan

1.   The _____ was characterized by a focus on law enforcement and crook catching.

2.   One of the earliest legal codes was carved in black stone basalt and is known as the laws of _____.

3.   The early American law enforcement agency that gained fame through the slaughter of Commanche peoples was the _____.

4.   _____ and _____ were London's first police commissioners.

5.   The _____ was characterized by an effort to remove politics from policing and to eliminate corruption.

6.   The first modern police force was the _____.

7.   The Metropolitan Police Act, which was introduced to Parliament in 1829, was introduced by _____.

8.   In Medieval England, _____ were charged with keeping the King's armaments in order if the need to defend or raid villages should arise.

9.   _____ advocated for change and spread awareness about social and criminal problems facing London and organized six people who agreed to serve as paid constables who were known as the _____.

10. Early American police services were performed by volunteer citizens who served on _____ or _____.

11. _____ was an early magistrate in London and advocated a formal, structured police force.

12. The _____ phase was characterized by the use of police and political corruption.

13. Civil unrest of the 1960s prompted police departments to return to a _____ model.

14. The _____ was originally created to assist mine owners in breaking coal strikes.

15. _____ were one effort used to implement police reform following the political entrenchment phase.

16. The _____ investigated and found wide spread corruption in the New York City Police Department in 1973.

Chapter 3
Personnel Systems

Chapter Outline

I.   Toward a Theory of Police Selection
II. Affirmative Action and Police Selection
    A. Title VII of the 1964 Civil Rights Act
    B. The Supreme Court: Lessening Title VII Requirements
    C. Minorities in Policing
    D. Women in Policing
    E. Recruiting Police Officers
    F. Establishing Minimum Selection Standards
        1. Residency Requirements
        2. Age Standards
        3. Vision Standards
        4. Educational Standards
        5. Physical Agility Standards
        6. Background and Work History
        7. Medical Standards
        8. Psychological Screening
III. The Police Selection Process
    A. The Written Test
    B. The Oral Interview Board
    C. The Assessment Center
IV. Training Police Officers
    A. Basic Training
    B. Field Training Officer (FTO) Programs
    C. In-Service Training
V.   Police Officer Career Development
    A. Lateral Expansion
    B. Vertical Expansion
VI. Impact of Race and Gender on Police Officer Careers

Key Concepts

Introduction
Recruiting, selecting, training, development, and retention of police officers are of critical importance to police departments. Departments could save millions of dollars annually through more judicious selection procedures. Police administrators must clearly articulate the goals of the organization, understand the roles and tasks to be performed, and ensure that the department's procedures select those who are capable of performing the tasks required of police officers.

Police Selection
Only the most qualified candidates should be promoted and hired, when doubt exists, the decision should be made in favor of the department. Federal and state laws and court decisions regulate how police agencies hire and promote employees. Title VII of the 1964 Civil Rights Act defined discrimination as the act of drawing distinctions from which to make selection and other personnel decisions based on considerations of race, color, sex, national origin, or religion. The primary methods for establishing discrimination in law enforcement were disparate rejection rates and population comparisons.

Minorities in Policing
Today, about 11.7 percent of the nation's police force is African-American. About 7.8 percent of the police force is Hispanic. The two primary reasons for under-representation of minorities in law enforcement are institutional barriers and personal preference. Bias, lack of recruiting strategies, discrimination, and sexual harassment are still problems for women in policing. About 10 percent of American police officers are female.

Recruiting Police Officers
Police recruitment is defined as the development of a pool of sufficiently qualified applicants from which to select officers. Selection standards are rooted in federal, state, and local laws and court decisions. They also reflect the department's concerns about what types of individuals can perform police work. Common selection criteria are: residency requirements, vision standards, educational standards, physical agility standards, background and work history, medical standards, and psychological screening.

The Police Selection Process
When a pool of acceptable applicants has been established, administrators attempt to select applicants who possess the qualities necessary to perform police duties at a high level. The process utilized is composed of many steps including: written test, physical agility test, polygraph tests, background or character investigation, medical examination, psychological evaluation, and oral interview.

Training Police Officers
Training is designed to offer selected applicants the knowledge and skills to perform police work. Training consists of three phases: basic training, field officer training, and in-service training.

Review of Key Terms

- assessment center
- *Bakke v. California*
- basic training
- *Davis v. Dallas*
- field officer training
- *Griggs v. Duke Power Co.*
- *Hild v. Bruner*
- in-service training
- lateral expansion
- medical standards
- physical agility standards
- polygraph
- psychological assessment
- residency requirements
- screen in
- selection standards
- Title VII of the 1964 Civil Rights Act
- vertical expansion
- written test

1. The **Polygraph** is used in an attempt to uncover information about an applicant's criminal history, drug and alcohol use, and ethics.

2. The three main objectives of **field officer training** are: (1) to reinforce learning that occurred in basic training; (2) to ensure that officers are able to apply those concepts; and (3) to provide more detailed information about specific aspects of the job.

3. Opponents of **residency requirements** argue that they restrict the applicant pool, thus reducing the overall quality of police selections.

4. **Medical standards** determine if an applicant is physically capable of performing the many tasks and responsibilities that are required of police officers.

5. Providing more opportunities for officers to advance within the department's rank structure is referred to as **vertical expansion**.

6. The **written test** is designed to measure an applicant's aptitude for police work and have historically been problematic for departments.

7. **Physical Agility Standards** are often tested in ways that are not related to the actual activities performed by police officers and have a detrimental effect on female applicants.

8.   Personnel systems should be designed to _Screen in_____ applicants to identify the most qualified applicants and make selections from a restricted pool.

9.   In _Bakke vs. California_ the court ruled that reverse discrimination was present when student openings were reserved for minorities.

10.   _Title VII_____ was the first federal legislative action taken in this country to prohibit discrimination in employment.

11.   In _Hild vs. Bruner_____ the court found a police department negligent for not performing a _psychological assessment_

12.   Title VII was not universally applied until _Griggs vs Power Co._ established new standards by which to judge the existence of discrimination in agencies.

13.   Training designed to keep veteran officers abreast of new or innovative procedures and techniques is referred to as _In Service training_

14.   There is very little uniformity in _selection standards_ across police departments.

15.   In _Davis vs Dallas_____ the court upheld a police department's 45 college hour entry requirement.

16.   The _assessment center_ consists of several tests, some of which are job simulations where candidates act out real situations from the job.

17.   _Basic training_____ is designed to provide officers with a rudimentary level of competency before entering into police work.

18.   Job specialization within a department increases with the size of the department and is referred to as _lateral expansion_ .

Chapter 4
Organization and Management

Chapter Outline

I.   The Specifics of Police Administration: POSDCORB
II.   Levels of Administration and Supervision
III.   Principles of Organization and Police Administration
     A.   Classical Organization Principles
         1.   Hierarchy
         2.   Specialization
         3.   Procedural Guidelines
         4.   Organizational Documentation
         5.   Organizational Authority
         6.   Appointment Based on Qualifications
     B.   Problems with Classical Organizational Principles and Traditional Police Administration
IV.   Human Relations Organizational Theory
     A.   The Hawthorne Studies
     B.   McGregor's Theory X and Theory Y
     C.   Maslow's Hierarchy of Needs
V.   Human Relations Theory and Police Administration
     A.   Participative Management
         1.   Vertical Staff Meetings
         2.   Problem-Solving Groups
         3.   Quality Circles
VI.   Systems Theory and Police Administration
     A.   Open Systems versus Closed Systems
     B.   Organizations as Systems
VII. Systems Theory and Policing
     A.   Management by Objectives (MBO)
     B.   Contingency Management
     C.   Total Quality Management
         1.   Culture
         2.   Customers
         3.   Counting

Key Concepts

Introduction
Organizations are distinguished by formal rules, division of labor, authority relationships, and limited or controlled membership. Organization refers to how a department is structured and shaped. Management refers to the processes that occur within the structure. The combination of organization and management embodies administration.

Specifics of Police Administration
Luther Gulick outlined POSDCORB, the activities that constitute administration. They are: Planning, Organizing, Staffing, Directing, Coordinating, Reporting, and Budgeting.

Principles of Organization and Police Administration
Max Weber was the first person to outline the principles of organization. His six principles are the foundation of classical organizational theory and are: hierarchy; specialization; policies and procedures; written rules; authority; and promotion based on qualification.

A less authoritarian approach to police organization is the human relations approach. This movement was prompted by the Hawthorne studies, McGregor's Theory X and Theory Y, and Maslow's Hierarchy of Needs. The focus of human relations theory is participative management, where the focus is on improving the internal workings of the department by allowing larger numbers of officers to be involved in decisionmaking. This is accomplished through vertical staff meetings, problem-solving groups, and quality circles.

Systems theory posits that organizations are a part of their environment and should closely monitor and react to changes in the environment and that administrators should view their organizations as systems. Systems can be open or closed, with open systems being viewed as total systems within an environment and closed systems making decisions without consideration of external factors.

Systems Theory and Policing
Systems theory, while more of a philosophy as opposed to a set of guidelines, has been implemented in a variety of forms. The three distinct forms that are most popular are: management by objectives, contingency management, and total quality management.

Review of Key Terms

classical organizational theory
contingency management
directing
Luther Gulick
Hawthorne studies
hierarchy
human relations theory
management
Management By Objectives
Maslow's Hierarchy of Needs
middle managers
organization
organizing
planning
POSDCORB
problem-solving groups
sergeants
specialization
Systems Theory
Theory X
Theory Y
vertical staff meetings
Max Weber

1. One implication of _____ is that the
    workplace provides an adequate financial reward to satisfy both physiological and
    safety needs and the work group generally satisfies the worker's need for
    belonging.

2. _____ dictates that administrators should view
    organizations as a complex set of pieces that must be coordinated, maintained, and
    controlled.

3. _____ assumes that there is no one best way to manage
    and that decisions should be based on the particulars of the problem under
    consideration.

4. Captains or lieutenants in larger departments are usually
    _____.

5. One principle of classical organizational theory is _____,
    which refers to chain of command.

6. One component of _____ is the idea that the average person will
    work as little as possible.

7. The continuous process of making decisions, developing policies and procedures is _____.

8. _____ refers to how a department is structured and shaped.

9. One form of participative management is _____ which includes representatives from all levels of the department.

10. _____ are the first-line supervisors in a police agency.

11. The movement toward a less authoritarian police management system was prompted by _____.

12. As departments grow in size, _____ or the development of units becomes necessary.

13. The activities of administration were first outlined by _____ and are referred to as _____.

14. One activity of administration is _____ and involves establishing a formal structure of units and people through which work is coordinated and accomplished.

15. The processes that occur within a structure are referred to as _____.

16. One activity of administration is _____ and includes developing a broad outline of what needs to be done and how the organization will accomplish the recognized purposes or objectives.

17. The foundation of _____, which is used in many police departments today, was first outlined by _____.

18. The _____ determined that increased productivity was caused by special attention being given to employees and was foundational for human relations theory.

19. One component of _____ is the idea that people are not passive or resistant to organizational needs.

20. Meetings that involve members from all levels of the department and focus on a single issue are referred to as _____.

21. The three valuable attributes that contribute to the success of _____ are: goals and goal setting, participation, and feedback.

Chapter 5
Police Operations

Chapter Outline

Key Concepts

Introduction

Police operations refer to the various police services provided citizens and the methods used by police agencies when delivering these services. Police services are delivered by a variety of operational units with the department, primarily: patrol, criminal investigation, and traffic. The patrol function is considered to be the most important operation of a law enforcement agency. The investigative functions focuses on solving crimes and the traffic function focuses on reducing accidents. The allocation of police personnel refers to making decisions about how many officers should be assigned to the various units in the police department.

Police Patrol

The patrol units are responsible for a variety of activities, including: deterring crime, enforcing laws, investigations, apprehending offenders, and writing reports among many others. Most departments establish beat boundaries and allocate patrol personnel accordingly. Various forms of patrol are utilized, including: automobile, foot, horse, bicycle, aircraft, and watercraft. Strategies of patrol include routine preventive patrol and directed patrol.

Criminal Investigations

The investigative functions focuses on solving crimes reported to the police. Historically, detectives have played many roles. Until the 1920s, detectives were "secretive rogues," alluding to the fact that they were often corrupt and involved in criminal activity. With the professionalization of policing came the detective as inquisitor, who used the "third degree" to solve crimes. The due process revolution of the 1960s placed legal constraints on investigations and detectives developed a bureaucratic role.

Preliminary investigations are initial inquires into a reported crime and are often conducted by a patrol unit. Follow-up or latent investigations are performed by detectives. These cases are of one of three types: walk-throughs, where-are-theys, and whodunits. Most cases are solved through specific suspect information provided by victims and witnesses.

The Traffic Function

The traffic function affects the most citizens. It is utilized to perform both the law enforcement and order-maintenance functions of the police. Proactive enforcement of traffic laws is designed to reduce the number and severity of accidents.

Police Paramilitary Units

Most police departments in the United States have paramilitary units (PPUs). These units are equipped with militaristic equipment and technology. They are structured after the military model and train under a military command structure. These units are primarily used to initiate an investigative raid on a residence, to serve a warrant, or conduct a drug investigation.

Review of Key Terms

bicycle patrol
differential police response
directed patrol
downtime
foot patrol
investigative function
Kansas City Patrol Study
patrol
police operations
police personnel
preliminary investigation
RAND study
routine preventive patrol
saturation patrol
secretive rogue
suspect-oriented techniques
traffic function
walk-through
where-are-they
whodunit

1. An initial inquiry into a reported crime that is often performed by patrol officers is a _____.

2. A _____ is a case in which a suspect has been identified and apprehended.

3. The _____ found that routine patrol has minimal effect on crime.

4. Officers in marked police vehicles perform _____ throughout an agency's jurisdiction.

5. The allocation of _____ refers to making decisions about how many officers should be assigned to the various units in the police department.

6. Agencies direct officers to concentrate on known suspects or classes of individuals when using _____.

7. One primary reason for the resurgence of _____foot patrol_____ was to address the problem of decreased citizen-officer interaction.

8. The various police services provided citizens and the methods used by police when delivering these services are referred to as _____.

9.   A case where the suspect has been identified but not apprehended is a
     _____ .

10. A _____ involves responding to citizen calls by
     means other than dispatching an officer.

11. The _____ function is responsible for enforcing laws, writing
     reports, maintaining order, and conflict resolution.

12. Departments utilize _____ in an effort to deter crime in a
     specific area by deploying large numbers of officers.

13. Any time an officer is committed to a call or police activity is referred to as
     _____ .

14. One advantage of _____ is that officers can travel a greater
     distance at a faster rate.

15. A _____ is a case where the preliminary investigation
     did not result in the identification of the perpetrator.

16. _____ consists of saturation patrol, stakeouts, surveillance
     and decoys.

17. The _____ centers around solving crimes known to
     police.

18. Early detectives were referred to as _____
     because they were often criminals and corrupt.

19. The _____ found that detectives did not generally solve
     cases by hard work, but focused on, and solved, easy cases.

20. The police _____ is both a law enforcement and an order-
     maintenance function.

Chapter 6
Police Discretion

Chapter Outline

Key Concepts

Introduction

Discretion is defined as the "when the effective limits on a public official's power leave him or her free to make a choice among a number of possible courses of action." All criminal justice system functionaries have and use discretion. Police officers use discretion on a daily basis. The qualities necessary for good use of discretion include: curiosity, ability to perceive danger, have a tragic perspective, be decisive, exercise self-control, and use varied approaches to unique problems.

Discretion can have positive and negative connotations. It holds the potential for abuse. Administrative discretion is exercised in determining the role orientation of the agency, in allocating officers to programs and geographic areas, in directing officers to focus on particular crimes, and attempting to control how officers perform their duties.

Departments attempt to control enforcement discretion by establishing policies and providing direction through orders and supervision.

The Police Decision-Making Process

As the "gatekeepers" of the criminal justice system, police officers make decisions about whether the criminal justice process with be initiated. The most important factor in this decision is the seriousness of the offense, but offender variables, situational variables, and system variables are also important. Offender variables include race, gender, and socioeconomic status. Situation variables include the interaction between officers and citizens, presence of a weapon, and visibility of the event. System variables include the system's capacity to prosecute and incarcerate those who commit crimes.

Situations that involve more discretion than others include domestic violence, vice crimes, hate crimes, and problems with disenfranchised populations.

Controlling Police Discretion

Control of police discretion is attempted through internal and external control mechanisms. Internal mechanisms refer to policies and guidelines implemented by departments to control officers' behavior. Training and supervision are also necessary.

External control mechanisms include citizen, legislative, and court controls.

Review of Key Terms

- administrative discretion
- civilian review boards
- discretion
- disenfranchised populations
- domestic violence
- enforcement discretion
- gatekeepers
- judgmental context
- legislative control
- offender variables
- prejudice
- situation variable
- system variables
- vice crime

1. Police are considered the _Gatekeepers_ of the criminal justice system because they determine who is subject to the criminal justice process.

2. Historically, police officers were detached and did not take action in situations involving _domestic violence_.

3. _Legislative Control_ includes the enactment of laws, the allocation of funds, and oversight.

4. The most important _situation variable_ that impacts the officer's decision making relates to the seriousness of the offense.

5. The decisions to enforce specific laws, to investigate crimes, to stop and search people, to arrest or detain an individual are all examples of _enforcement discretion_

6. The _judgemental context_ refers to whether discretionary decisions should be made in a certain situation.

7. _Prejudice_ is a reflection of one's values and attitudes that develop through the socialization process.

8. _Civilian Review Boards_ were created to maintain effective discipline of the police, provide satisfactory resolution of citizen complaints, maintain citizen confidence in the police and influence police administrators.

9. The idiosyncrasies of the criminal justice system that may influence officers exercising their discretion are referred to as _system variables_.

10. Criminal activity that is against the public order or public morality and includes prostitution, gambling, and pornography is referred to as _vice crime_.

11.   An officer uses __discretion__ when the effective limits on power leave him/her free to make a choice among a number of possible courses of action.

12.   The determination of the role orientation of an agency is an example of __administrative discretion__

13.   Race, gender, and socioeconomic status can impact police decisionmaking and are examples of __offender variables__

14.   The mentally ill, public inebriates, and the homeless are examples of __disenfranchised populations__

Chapter 7
Police Use of Force

Chapter Outline

Key Concepts

The Meaning of Excessive Force

There is much disagreement when a use of force incident occurs as to whether the force was excessive. The three criteria that best determines excessive force are: (1) criminal law, (2) civil liability, and (3) fear of scandal. Excessive force differs from excessive use of force. Excessive force is present when an officer applies too much force in a specific situation. Excessive use of force is when an officer legally applies force in too many incidents. Excessive force can be "extralegal violence" or "brutality."

Tennessee v. Garner

In 1985, the U.S. Supreme Court ruled in *Tennessee v. Garner* that officers cannot use deadly force on a fleeing felon to effect an arrest. The suspect must present harm to the officer or the community. In essence, the ruling struck down the "fleeing felon doctrine."

Patterns of Police Use of Force

An overwhelming majority of police/citizen contacts do not involve any force. The most common type of force involves handcuffs. Slightly more than one-half of the victims on the police force are minorities and 80 percent are males. Police kill an average of 373 citizens each year. Use of force by off-duty officers presents special problems for departments, and much debate surrounds the decision to arm off-duty officers.

Problem Officers

Studies have indicated that departments sometimes have problem officers. These officers are more likely to be involved in problematic use of force situations. Early warning systems have been developed to identify these officers and look for: complaints, use of force, reprimands, and discharge of firearms.

Less-Than-Lethal Force

Departments have attempted to reduce injury to citizens by utilizing alternative weapons. The introduction of these weapons, (i.e., pepper spray, rubber bullets, and tear gas) have not decreased the incidence of force. Some researchers have argued that these weapons have lead to "net-widening" or officers using force when they would not have otherwise done so.

Assaults Against Police Officers

An average of 79 police officers are killed in the line of duty each year. This number has decreased in recent years due to citizens being less likely to use force, increased use of body armor, and officers receiving better emergency medical care.

Review of Key Terms

CALEA
deadly force
early warning systems
excessive force
excessive use of force
less-than-lethal force
net-widening
off-duty use of force
Oleoresin Capsicum Spray
soft handed force
suicide by cop
Tennessee v. Garner
use of force continuum

1.   The idea that officers possessing less-than-lethal weapons may be more inclined to use force in cases where they would not have been legally justified using traditional weapons is referred to as _____.

2.   _____ is a victim precipitated homicide where the victim takes action that causes the police to use deadly force.

3.   When an officer physically grabs a suspect to control him/her, it is referred to as _____.

4.   _____ is the organization that oversees the national accreditation of police agencies.

5.   _____ is present when an officer applies too much force in a specific situation.

6.   Many departments have developed _____ in an effort to identify problem officers.

7.   When an officer discharges a service firearm, it is considered to be _____.

8.   _____ has become one of the primary weapons used by the police to subdue suspects.

9.   The U.S. Supreme Court ruled in _____ that officers cannot use deadly force against a fleeing felon.

10. Many police departments have adopted a _____ to outline the level of force officers can use when subduing suspects.

11.   When an officer applies force in too many incidents it is referred to as
_____ .

12.   Alcohol is often involved in _____ situations.

13.   In an effort to save lives and avoid negative criticism, many departments have
begun to utilize _____ weapons.

Chapter 8
Police Culture and Behavior

Chapter Outline

Key Concepts

Perspectives of Police Culture and Behavior

Police roles and functions set officers apart from other members of society. The police as an occupational group can be distinguished from other members in society. The three different views that facilitate understanding of police behaviors and culture are: psychological, sociological, and anthropological. The psychological perspective focuses on predetermined personality characteristics of those entering law enforcement. The sociological perspective assumes that police officers learn their social personality from training and through exposure to police work and includes various typologies of police behavior. The anthropological perspective assumes that officers are influenced and shaped by their culture. This view of police behavior is termed a culturalization model.

The Police Subculture

Culture is the entire array of human symbols and artifacts, especially the meaning and value assigned to them. A primary distinction between American culture in general and the police occupational subculture is the law. Police officers have a legal monopoly on the sanctioned use of violence against other members of society. Law shapes police perceptions of events, situations, and self-image.

The Police World View

A cultural world view is the manner in which a culture sees the world and its own role and relationship to the world. Therefore, various social groups perceive the world, people, and situations differently from other social groups. Officer socialization creates a "we-they" world view, an us-against-them mentality. Danger and authority are inherent in the development of this view.

Police Ethos

The concept of ethos encompasses the fundamental spirit of a culture. It is sentiments, beliefs, customs, and practices. The police ethos includes bravery, autonomy, and secrecy.

Police Themes

Themes in a cultures are related to the belief systems or "dynamic affirmations" maintained by its members. The theme of isolation is important to policing. Police officers impose social isolation upon themselves as a means of protection against real and perceived dangers. Solidarity is another theme and relates to being loyal and a sense of alliance with other officers.

Police Postulates

Postulates are statements of belief held by a culture that reflect its basic orientations. They are less formal than themes and are expressions of general truth or principles accepted by a subculture.

Police Stress

Police stress exists, but there is much disagreement on its sources, consequences, and extent. Davis Carter's typology of sources of police stress includes: life-threatening, social isolation, organizational, functional, personal, physiological, and psychological stressors. Stress also affects police officers' families and spouses. There is little conclusive evidences to indicate that police stress leads to a higher rate of suicides among officers. Studies have conflicted on whether or not police officers have higher rates of drug and alcohol abuse, mortality resulting from heart disease and diabetes, and developing colon and liver cancers.

Review of Key Terms

— anthropological perspective
authoritarian personality
community service officer
— culture
— ethos
functional stressors
— isolation
— legalistic-abuse officer
— life-threatening stressors
— postulates
— problem solver
— professionalization
— psychological perspective
— social isolation stressors
— solidarity
task officers
themes
— tough cops
— world view

1. Statements of belief held by a culture that reflect its basic orientations are referred to as postulates .

2. The entire array of human symbols and artifacts and the meaning and value assigned to them form a groups' culture .

3. Subcultural sentiments, beliefs, customs, and practices combine to form the police ethos .

4. Life threatening stressors are characterized by the constant potential of injury or death.

5. A tough cop views his/her job as keeping criminals under control and uses very repressive methods.

6. The two dominant themes in the police subculture are isolation and solidarity .

7. The police world view is best described as a "we-they" or "us-them" orientation.

8. A legalistic-abuse officer is one who typically views his/her role as the protectors of the "right" moral standards.

9. The process by which norms and values are internalized as workers begin to learn their new occupation is referred to as professionalization

10. The _psychological perspective_ assumes that people with certain types of personalities enter law enforcement and behave in certain ways.

11. _Problem solver_ is an officer who is more sympathetic to people's needs and views people as clients, not adversaries.

12. Alienation from the community, cynicism, and prejudice are forms of _social isolation stressors_

13. The _anthropological perspective_ of police behavior assumes that officers are influenced and shaped by their culture and that beliefs and values are transmitted from one generation of officers to the next.

14. _Task officers_ are those who follow departmental rules and regulations without exception.

15. The _authoritarian personality_ is characterized by conservative, aggressive, cynical, and rigid behavior.

16. The _community service officer_ uses discretion liberally and has a primary objective of helping people.

17. _Themes_ help shape the quality and structure of the group's social interactions and are related to the belief systems of the groups members.

18. _Functional stressors_ are specifically related to the performance of assigned policing duties.

Chapter 9
Ethics and Deviance

Chapter Outline

I.   Sources of Ethics
    A.   Justice
    B.   Law
    C.   Agency Policy
    D.   Professional Code of Ethics
    E.   Social Norms and Personal Values
    F.   A Conflict of Values
II. Crime, Corruption, Abuse, and Illegal Behavior
    A.   Police Crime
    B.   Abuse of Authority
    C.   Occupational Deviance
    D.   Corruption
        1.   Bribery
        2.   Extortion
        3.   Narcotics Violations
        4.   Scope and Forms of Police Corruption
III. Deviant Behavior
    A.   Alcohol and Other Drugs of Abuse
    B.   Sexual Misconduct
    C.   Police Sexual Violence
    D.   Driving While Black
    E.   Gratuities
    F.   Goldbricking versus Quotas

Key Concepts

Ethics

Ethics is a concept that is difficult to define. For some it is a question on consequences, if the end result is good for the greatest number of people the action is moral. If the end result is bad, the action is immoral. This cannot be the standard for police officers as it opens the door to many illegal and unconstitutional practices. Deontological ethics does not consider consequences, but examines one's duty to act.

Sources of Ethics

Police officers rely on many sources for guidance in making decisions. These include: the concept of justice, laws, agency policies, codes of ethics, social norms, and personal values.

Crime, Corruption, Abuse, and Illegal Behavior

The initial focus on police ethics centered around conduct that was illegal. Officers who commit crimes are often called "corrupt." For many, any crime committed by an officer is a sign of a corrupt officer, however, there is debate over this issue. Police abuse of authority includes actions that "tread on human dignity... or violate an inherent legal right of a member of the police constituency."

Police occupational deviance refers to inappropriate work-related activities in which police may participate, but must include the misuse of the officer's authority. Police corruption involves the misuse of authority for personal gain. Common corrupt behaviors include: bribery, extortion, and drug violations.

Scope and Forms of Police Corruption

A long tradition of hopeless corruption and brutality lead to the development of investigative commissions. The Knapp Commission investigated the New York City police department in 1970. Its report, two years later, concluded that corruption was widespread in the department. The Commission identified "meat eaters" and "grass eaters." Meat eaters aggressively pursued corrupt activities, while grass eaters engaged in illegal activity occasionally when the opportunity presented itself.

Corrupt Departments

Departments can be classified according to the amount and type of corruption. A typology of corrupt departments was developed by Sherman and includes: Type I, Rotten Apples and Rotten Pockets which has individual officers who use their position for personal gain. Type II, Pervasive Unorganized Corruption includes individual behavior that is not effectively controlled or organized. Type III, Pervasive Organized Corruption includes corruption when officers act in an organized manner.

Deviant Behavior

Deviant behavior occurs when an officer violates the norms or rules of conduct expected of a member of the police profession. It can be legal or illegal behavior that is committed on or off duty. Common behaviors include: use of alcohol and other drugs, sexual misconduct, racial profiling, accepting gratuities, and goldbricking.

Review of Key Terms

abuse of authority
bribery
corruption
deviant behavior
disrespect
due process
extortion
goldbricking
grass-eaters
gratuities
justice
law
loyalty
meat-eaters
morality
occupational deviance
pervasive organized corruption
professional code of ethics
Rotten Apples
socialization
utilitarianism

1. An officer who uses the threat of arrest or harassment when requiring something of value from a citizen is guilty of *extortion*.

2. When an officer avoids work or performs only the amount necessary to satisfy supervisors, it is called *goldbricking*.

3. The most problematic type of corruption is in departments characterized as having *persuasive organized deviance* because officers act in an organized manner.

4. New officers are taught by veterans that *loyalty* is an officer's most important duty and includes protecting fellow officers.

5. A *grass eater* is a corrupt officer who engages in illegal activities only occasionally or when circumstances of their work presents the opportunity.

6. For some, the term *morality* denotes the capacity of people to make judgments about what is right or good.

7. New police officers are taught that *disrespect* for police authority should be punished by arrest or the use of force.

8. When a citizen initiates an offer of something of value to influence an officer's performance of official duty, it is considered to be *bribery*.

9. An agency that has individual officers who commit corrupt acts on an individual basis is classified as having _Rotten apples_ .

10. _Abuse of authority_ is any action by an officer without regard to motive that injures, insults, or treads on human dignity, and/or violates an inherent legal right of a citizen.

11. One source of police ethics that drives police behavior yet is very difficult to define is _justice_ .

12. _Occupational deviance_ refers to inappropriate work-related activities, criminal and noncriminal, committed in the course of normal work activities or under the guise of authority.

13. The idea that we judge the correctness of an action by its outcome or consequences refers to _utilitarianism_ .

14. _Law_ is a source of police ethics that controls the behavior of individuals but also provides a way for citizens to control the government.

15. _Deviant behavior_ occurs when an officer violates the norms or rules of conduct expected of a member of the police profession.

16. A _prof. codes of conduct_ guides and restricts the behavior of members of a professional group.

17. The process of _socialization_ teaches individuals which behaviors are considered appropriate.

18. A _meat-eater_ is a corrupt officer who aggressively pursues corrupt activities.

19. Veteran officers teach new officers that _due process_ only protects criminals and can by bypassed when necessary to solve a crime.

20. _Corruption_ is defined as the misuse of authority for personal gain.

21. Coffee, food, and other items or services given to police officers for a reduced price or at no charge are referred to as _gratuities_ .

Chapter 10
Civil Liability

Chapter Outline

Key Concepts

Civil Liability

The duties and tasks of police officers are further complicated by lawsuits. Civil suits against the police are not always the product of their inability or failure to perform duties, sometimes they involve misconduct and abuses of authority. There has been an increase in the number of civil suits filed against police agencies since the 1960s. The average jury award of liability against a municipality is about $2 million. There is also a growing trend to settle these cases out of court.

Police Civil Liability and Tort Law

Torts are legal actions between private parties that do not arise form written contracts. They can be: strict liability or intentional. The most common forms of intentional tort actions against police officers are wrongful death, false arrest, false imprisonment, and assault and battery.

Negligence

Negligence is inadvertent behavior that results in damage or injury. Four elements that must be shown before an officer can be found liable for a claim of negligence are: (1) a legal duty; (2) a breach of that duty; (3) proximate causation; and (4) actual damage or injury. The most common claims of negligence include: negligent operation of emergency vehicles; failure to protect; failure to arrest; failure to render assistance; selection, hiring, and retention; supervision and direction; entrustment and assignment; and failure to discipline and investigate.

Defenses to Claims of Police Negligence

The most common defenses to negligence include: contributory negligence, comparative negligence, and assumption of the risk.

Police Liability Under Federal Law

The Civil Rights Act of 1871 was enacted by Congress to control the behavior of state officials and allow legal redress to those people whose constitutional rights were violated. The Act was codified as Title 42 of the U.S. code, Section 1983. It allows people whose civil rights are violated by government officials to bring civil suit in federal court to recover damages. In order to do this, the person must show: (1) the officials were acting under color of state law, and (2) the alleged violation was of a constitutional or federally protected right.

Defenses to Section 1983 Lawsuits

The defenses utilized by police officers in Section 1983 lawsuits all serve to limit and/or eliminate the recovery of damages by the plaintiff. The four primary defenses are: (1) absolute immunity, (2) qualified immunity, (3) probable cause, and (4) good faith.

Review of Key Terms

absolute immunity
acting under color of state law
assault
comparative negligence
contributory negligence
defendant
false arrest
intentional tort action
legal duty
liability litigation
negligence
negligent failure to arrest
negligent failure to discipline and investigate
negligent failure to protect
negligent police supervision and direction
plaintiff
qualified immunity
Section 1983
strict tort liability
torts
wrongful death

1.   Behaviors recognized by courts that require police officers to take action or to refrain from taking action in a particular situation involves

      _____.

2.   Actions brought under _____ must involve the violation of a constitutionally or federally protected right.

3.   An officer who injures someone by failing to enforce the law can be guilty of

      _____.

4.   In an _____ the plaintiff must prove that the defendant's behavior was intended to cause damage or injury.

5.   To prove _____, the plaintiff must establish that they were willfully, unwillfully or unlawfully detained.

6.   A police department that fails to provide effective systems of police accountability can be guilty of _____.

7.   A civil action brought against a person protected by _____ will be dismissed.

8.   A defense available to police officers that focuses on reducing the amount of the damage award is _____.

9. A _____ is a legal action between private parties that do not arise from written contracts.

10. _____ is inadvertent behavior that results in damage or injury.

11. Off-duty police officers who perform police functions can be considered to be _____.

12. Claims of _____ often arise as a result of police use of deadly force, which can be intentional or negligent.

13. Unlike criminal trials, _____ is tried in civil court and involves a _____ who claims injury, and a _____ who is allegedly responsible for the injury.

14. Police officers who are performing duties of a discretionary nature are often protected by _____.

15. A common defense for police officers is _____ which attempts to show that the plaintiff was also negligent in causing the damage or injury.

16. Behavior that is considered to be so dangerous that a reasonable person who engages in such behavior can be certain the conduct will result in injury or damage usually involves _____.

17. Behavior that inflicts injury or causes a person to fear the infliction of immediate injury is an _____.

18. When a police officer fails to take adequate actions to protect a person from a known and foreseeable danger, it can be deemed _____.

19. A police department that fails to provide effective systems of evaluation, control, and monitoring of employees' performances can be guilty of _____.

Chapter 11
The Police in the Modern Community

Chapter Outline

I. Introduction
II. An Overview of Public Perceptions of the Police
    A. Public Attitudes Toward the Police
    B. Individual-Level Variables
        1. Age
        2. Race
        3. Gender
        4. Socioeconomic Status
        5. Criminal Victimization
III. Police Community Relations
    A. Toward a Theory of Police-Community Relations
        1. The Public Relations Model
        2. Police-Community Relations Units
        3. The Organizational Change Model
IV. Crime Prevention
    A. The Theory of Crime Prevention
    B. Primary Crime Prevention Techniques and Programs
        1. Environmental Design
        2. Neighborhood Watches
        3. Public Education
    C. Juvenile Curfews
    D. Private Security
    E. Community Policing
    F. The Philosophical Dimension
        1. Broad Police Function
        2. Citizen Input
        3. Neighborhood Variation
    G. The Strategic Dimension
        1. Geographical Focus
        2. Prevention Focus
        3. Substantive Focus
    H. The Programmatic Dimension
        1. Reoriented Police Operations
        2. Problem-Solving and Situational Crime Prevention
        3. Community Engagement
    I. Management Issues
    J. Operational Examples

Key Concepts

Introduction

While the police depend on citizens to report crimes and provide information, the relationship between the two is often strained. In general, citizens view the police positively, but this changes some depending on certain demographic characteristics. Most researchers have reviewed public attitudes based on race, age, gender, and socioeconomic status.

Police-Community Relations

There are three primary models police have utilized in effort to strengthen community relations. They include: (1) the public relations model; (2) the police-community relations unit model; and (3) the organizational change model. The public relations model attempts to change attitudes toward police by highlighting the many and varied responsibilities that officers perform. The police-community relations unit model involves sending specialized units to areas that have the greatest problems with the police. The third model, the organizational change model, attempts to make changes in the way the departments and officers view and interact with disenfranchised portions of the community.

Crime Prevention

The police came to focus on crime prevention as the result of much civil unrest in the 1960s. It was warmly accepted by the middle and upper classes and is a primary focus of police departments across the country. There are three primary approaches to crime prevention: (1) primary; (2) secondary; and (3) tertiary. Primary crime prevention attempts to identify and manage conditions in the social and physical environment that provide opportunities for crime. Secondary crime prevention focuses on people and the community in an effort to identify potential criminals and high crime areas. Tertiary crime prevention deals with people who have committed criminal acts.

Some common crime prevention programs include: environmental design, surveillance, neighborhood watches, public education, and juvenile curfews.

Community Policing

The three major dimensions present when community policing is implemented are: (1) the philosophical dimension, (2) the strategic dimension, and (3) the programmatic dimension. The philosophical dimension involves a broad police function, citizen input, and neighborhood variation. The strategic dimension involves a geographical focus, a prevention focus, and a substantive focus. The programmatic dimension involves: reoriented police operations, problem-solving and situational crime prevention, and community engagement.

Review of Key Terms

access control
broad police function
environmental design
geographic focus
individual level variables
organizational change model
police-community relations unit
primary crime prevention
problem solving
public education
public relations model
secondary crime prevention
situational crime prevention
surveillance
tertiary crime prevention

1.   Departments that utilize _____ as opportunity-reducing measures believe that crime is a product of "rational choice."

2.   The _____ technique of community policing involves identifying a problem, analyzing it, identifying solutions, and implementing and evaluating these solutions.

3.   Effort that attempt to prevent "known criminals" from committing more crime are examples of _____.

4.   Physical changes designed to increase the potential for observation of criminal activity are referred to as _____.

5.   A _____ is a specialized division within a department that devotes its time and resources toward improving relations with the community.

6.   Police efforts that focus on people and the community in an effort to identify potential criminals and high-crime areas are examples of _____.

7.   Age, race, and gender are _____ that can impact perceptions of the police.

8.   Efforts designed to make criminal activity more difficult or to enhance apprehension are examples of _____.

9.   The notion of "defensible space" led to _____ as a form of crime prevention.

10. Police administrators using the _____ believe that they have to educate the public about the police in order to improve relations.

11. Community policing calls for a _____ that includes fear reduction, order maintenance, and crime fighting.

12. Departments operating under the _____ alter the department's structure or attitudes in an effort to enhance community relations.

13. The physical changes that are made to inhibit or control the flow of people into or out of an area are examples of _____.

14. One aspect of community policing that involves officers working in the same area on a permanent basis is referred to as _____.

15. Police departments use _____ to overcome negative community relations.

Chapter 12
Policing the Drug Problem

Chapter Outline

Key Concepts

The Nature of the Drug Problem

The current war on drugs began in earnest in 1969 and has continued with subsequent Presidential administrations. Law enforcement agencies at the federal, state, and local levels are involved in fighting the war on drugs. The strategies in this war do not target illicit drugs, they target users of these substances. About 35 percent of Americans over age 12 have used an illegal drug. Marijuana is the illicit drug of choice among Americans.

Drugs and Crime

Most addicts who commit crimes to support their habits committed crime prior to using drugs. Research indicates that a majority of arrestees in certain cities are under the influence of drugs at the time of arrest. While this tells us little about whether or not they are guilty of the crime, or were using drugs at the time of commission, these studies indicate that most test positive for marijuana. Violence associated with drugs emanates from the illegality of the substances, not the pharmacological effects of the drugs. Violence associated with drugs is: (1) psychopharmacological, which relates to the ingestion of a substance; (2) Economic compulsive, which relates to committing crimes to get money to buy drugs; and (3) System, which involves violence resulting from the "business" of drugs.

The Nations Drug Strategy

One strategy in the war on drugs is interdiction, preventing drugs from entering the country. Some strategies focus on prevention, or attempts to keep people, especially children, from experimenting with drugs. Drug education and treatment programs are also utilized.

Illegal Drug Delivery System

Drugs are imported into and manufactured in the United States. This is done by criminal organizations. Colombian drug cartels are the most widely known. La Cosa Nostra, Jamaican Posses, Outlaw Motorcycle Gangs, and street gangs also traffic drugs.

Drug Enforcement Techniques and Programs

Police have utilized various strategies in the war on drugs, all with varying levels of success. One technique involves attacking high-level drug "kingpins." This often involves asset forfeiture. Retail level enforcement strategies are the responsibility of local and state law enforcement. These focus on the people conducting drug transactions at the local level. These programs often involve street sweeps, neighborhood crackdowns, neighborhood involvement, and third party policing. Community policing has offered a variety of initiatives in the war on drugs. These programs usually involve the community in some way and focus heavily on nontraditional methods.

Review of Key Terms

behavioral model
Border Patrol
citywide street sweeps
Colombian drug cartels
cultural gangs
drug prevention
economic compulsive
entrepreneurial gangs
interdiction
La Cosa Nostra
moral model
neighborhood crackdowns
Operation Intercept
Outlaw motorcycle gangs
Psychopharmacological
self-medication model
street gangs
systemic violence
third party policing

1.   Gangs that form for the purpose of forming a criminal enterprise are referred to as
      entreprenureal gangs

2.   The primary focus of *street gangs* is the sale of crack and
      cocaine.

3.   The *moral model* attempts to explain drug addiction by attributing
      drug use to people who are bad.

4.   *Colombian drug cartels* are some of the most successful drug trafficking
      organizations with operative networks in Florida, California, and New York.

5.   Violence resulting from a decreased mental capacity associated with the use of an
      illicit substance is referred to as *psychphamacological*

6.   The drug trafficking organization that is usually described as a "family" is
      La Cosa Nostra .

7.   The trafficking of methamphetamines in the United States is the primary business
      of *outlaw motorcycle gangs*

8.   Increased police activity in target areas that are designed to suppress the street
      drug market are called *citywide street sweeps*

9.   The *self-medication model* attempts to explain drug addiction by
      defining addiction as a symptom of some mental defect.

10. When police attack a drug problem by engaging other parties who have a vested interest in the activity it is referred to as *third party policing*

11. Strategies that attempt to prevent illicit drugs from entering the border are forms of *interdiction* .

12. Gangs that view drug dealing as a means to achieve social goals are often referred to as *cultural gangs* .

13. Violence for the purpose of getting money to support an addiction is referred to as *economic compulsive*

14. One agency involved in interdiction programs is the *Border patrol* .

15. The program that began the first war on drugs in 1969 was called *operation intercept*

16. *Systematic violence* results from the "business" of illegal drugs.

17. *Drug prevention* programs are basically education programs that are designed to keep people from using illicit drugs.

18. The *behavioral model* of drug addiction focuses on drug use as a learned behavior that involves peer pressure and other social contacts.

19. Concentrated, long-term police attention given to an area identified as a "hot spot" is called a *neighborhood crackdown*

Chapter 13
The Future of Policing

Chapter Outline

I.   Predictions for the Future Police Roles and Functions
    A.   Police Roles and Functions
    B.   Political and Legal Change
    C.   Technology and the Police
II.   Managing Information and Communication with Enhanced Technology
    A.   Communications
    B.   Computers, Communication, and Information
    C.   Computer Software
    D.   Information Systems
III.   Technology for Field Operations
    A.   Automated Traffic Enforcement
    B.   Video Cameras
    C.   Investigation and Crime Scene Technology

Key Concepts

Introduction

Most predictions of the future are made based on what has occurred in the past. The future of policing is dependent on shifting social and political trends that directly affect policing.

Predictions for the Future

The leading scholars who attempt to predict the future of policing are William Tafoya and Georgette Bennett. Tafoya predicts that law enforcement will shift to a service philosophy, while Bennett predicts a less personal law enforcement role. Others predict an increase in militarizing law enforcement, especially related to the war on drugs.

Political and Legal Change

The conservative nature of law and the police will slow social change. Methods of dealing with crime and social problems are restricted and will also slow change. It is likely that civil liberties will be curbed in an effort to reduce crime. Technology will play a role in the future of policing.

Managing Information and Communication with Enhanced Technology

Some of the greatest changes in law enforcement may be in the areas of communication and information management. The greatest impact can be found in the sharing of information between departments. Computers will impact radio traffic and writing reports. Crime mapping has and will continue to impact policing, especially the identification of "hot spots."

Technology for Field Operations

Automated traffic enforcement devices, which involve photographing violators and producing a citation with very little human activity, are already being used by some departments. The primary shift in this practice is likely to involve privatization. Video and digital recording devices are also being used for recording crime scenes, or recording from patrol cars. It is also likely that DNA will play an enhanced role in investigations.

Review of Key Terms

- automated traffic enforcement
- civil disorder
- communication
- Computer-Assisted Report Entry (CARE)
- crime mapping
- DNA
- Georgette Bennett
- Militarization
- mobile data terminals
- social arrangements
- William Tafoya
- video recording

1. Some departments are currently using *CARE* in an effort to reduce the time officers spend writing reports.

2. One primary role of police relates to maintaining existing *social arrangements* through the use of force if necessary.

3. The United States Supreme Court has allowed *video recording* in the prosecution of suspected drunk drivers.

4. Some scholars have predicted that an increased *militarization* will occur in modern policing as a result of the war on drugs.

5. *Automated traffic enforcement* involves unmarked cars containing a camera and a radar device parked along the roadway.

6. One prediction made by *William Tafoya* relates to a shift from a legalistic orientation to a service philosophy as the dominant style of policing.

7. As technology becomes available to police agencies, *communication* between departments is enhanced.

8. One prediction made by *Georgette Bennett* involves less personal tactics and a focus on the law enforcement role.

9. Identification of "problem" neighborhoods and "hot spots" is done through *crime mapping* .

10. The most compelling use of scientific inquiry is *DNA* fingerprinting, which will assist in the identification of suspects.

11. Tafoya has predicted that *civil disorder* will plague America because of the way our society addresses social change.

12. _Mobil data terminals_ are currently being used by police departments so that officers can make clear and accurate reports at a crime scene from their vehicles.

Answers

Chapter 1
Review of Key Terms

1. federalism
2. service style
3. Bureau of Alcohol, Tobacco, and Firearms
4. civil law
5. democratic systems
6. watchman style
7. case law
8. separation of powers
9. constitution
10. legalistic style
11. procedural law
12. crime control model
13. society; government
14. U.S. Marshal Service
15. substantive law
16. due process model

Chapter 2
Review of Key Terms

1. professional era
2. Hammurabi
3. Texas Rangers
4. Charles Rowan; Richard Mayne
5. reform era
6. London Metropolitan Police Force
7. Sir Robert Peel
8. constables
9. Henry Fielding; Bow Street Runners
10. slave patrols; Night Watches
11. Patrick Colquhoun
12. political entrenchment
13. community relations
14. Pennsylvania State Police
15. investigative commissions
16. KNAPP commission

Chapter 3
Review of Key Terms

1. polygraph
2. field officer training
3. residency requirements
4. medical standards
5. vertical expansion
6. written test
7. physical agility standards
8. screen in
9. *Bakke v. California*
10. Title VII of the 1964 Civil Rights Act
11. *Hild v. Bruner*; psychological assessment
12. *Griggs v. Duke Power Co.*
13. in-service training
14. selection standards
15. *Davis v. Dallas*
16. assessment center
17. basic training
18. lateral expansion

Chapter 4
Review of Key Terms

1. Maslow's Hierarchy of Needs
2. systems theory
3. contingency management
4. middle managers
5. hierarchy
6. Theory X
7. directing
8. organization
9. vertical staff meetings
10. sergeants
11. human relations theory
12. specialization
13. Luther Gulick; POSDCORB
14. organizing
15. management
16. planning
17. classical organizational theory; Max Weber
18. Hawthorne studies
19. Theory Y
20. problem-solving groups
21. Management By Objectives

Chapter 5
Review of Key Terms

1. preliminary investigation
2. walk-through
3. Kansas City Patrol Study
4. routine preventive patrol
5. police personnel
6. suspect-oriented techniques
7. foot patrol
8. police operations
9. where-are-they
10. differential police response
11. patrol
12. saturation patrol
13. downtime
14. bicycle patrol
15. whodunit
16. directed patrol
17. investigative function
18. secretive rogues
19. RAND study
20. traffic function

Chapter 6
Review of Key Terms

1. gatekeepers
2. domestic violence
3. legislative control
4. situation variable
5. enforcement discretion
6. judgmental context
7. prejudice
8. civilian review boards
9. system variables
10. vice crime
11. discretion
12. administrative discretion
13. offender variables
14. disenfranchised populations

Chapter 7
Review of Key Terms

1.   net-widening
2.   suicide by cop
3.   soft handed
4.   CALEA
5.   excessive force
6.   early warning systems
7.   deadly
8.   Oleoresin Capsicum Spray
9.   *Tennessee v. Garner*
10. use of force continuum
11. excessive use of force
12. off-duty use of force
13. less-than-lethal force

Chapter 8
Review of Key Terms

1.   postulates
2.   culture
3.   ethos
4.   life-threatening stressors
5.   tough cop
6.   isolation; solidarity
7.   world view
8.   legalistic-abuse officer
9.   professionalization
10. psychological perspective
11. problem solver
12. social isolation stressors
13. anthropological perspective
14. task officers
15. authoritarian personality
16. community service officer
17. themes
18. functional stressors

Chapter 9
Review of Key Terms

1.   extortion
2.   goldbricking
3.   pervasive organized corruption
4.   loyalty

5. grass-eater
6. morality
7. disrespect
8. bribery
9. rotten apples
10. abuse of authority
11. justice
12. occupational deviance
13. utilitarianism
14. law
15. deviant behavior
16. professional code of ethics
17. socialization
18. meat-eater
19. due process
20. corruption
21. gratuities

Chapter 10
Review of Key Terms

1. legal duty
2. Section 1983
3. negligent failure to arrest
4. intentional tort action
5. false arrest
6. negligent failure to discipline and investigate
7. absolute immunity
8. comparative negligence
9. tort
10. negligence
11. acting under color of state law
12. wrongful death
13. liability litigation, plaintiff, defendant
14. qualified immunity
15. contributory negligence
16. strict tort liability
17. assault
18. negligent failure to protect
19. negligent police supervision and direction

Chapter 11
Review of Key Terms

1. situational crime prevention
2. problem solving
3. tertiary crime prevention
4. surveillance
5. police-community relations unit
6. secondary crime prevention
7. individual level variables
8. primary crime prevention
9. environmental design
10. public relations model
11. broad police function
12. organizational change model
13. access control
14. geographic focus
15. public education

Chapter 12
Review of Key Terms

1. entrepreneurial gangs
2. street gangs
3. moral model
4. Colombian drug cartels
5. psychopharmacological
6. La Cosa Nostra
7. outlaw motorcycle gangs
8. citywide street sweeps
9. self-medication model
10. third party policing
11. interdiction
12. cultural gangs
13. economic compulsive
14. Border Patrol
15. Operation Intercept
16. systemic violence
17. drug prevention
18. behavioral model
19. neighborhood crackdown

Chapter 13
Review of Key Terms

1. Computer-Assisted Report Entry (CARE)
2. social arrangements
3. video recording
4. militarization
5. automated traffic enforcement
6. William Tafoya
7. communication
8. Georgette Bennett
9. crime mapping
10. DNA
11. civil disorder
12. mobile data terminals